1 Which of thes

stick to a magnet?

a tick.

Make a list of some other **magnetic** materials.

1) ____________________ 2) ____________________

3) ____________________ 4) ____________________

5) ____________________ 6) ____________________

2 Think about the three words **transparent** (1), **translucent** (2) and **opaque** (3).
Now write 1, 2 or 3 against these objects.

Think of some more transparent, translucent or opaque objects.

1) ____________________

2) ____________________

3) ____________________

3 Some of the things we throw away eventually rot. We say they are **biodegradable**. Tick the objects below that are biodegradable.

Why is it wrong to throw away **non-biodegradable** things?

____

____

____

4 Which, out of each pair, will produce the higher note when **struck** or **plucked**.
Tick the ones that make the **higher** notes.

Why do you think this is so?

____

____

____

5 Look at the two **circuits** below. In which one will the bulbs be brighter?

Can you say why?

____

____

____

6 Look at these circuits. If the switch is connected to **A**, then **B**, then **C**, which piece of equipment will be activated each time? Will it be the **bell**, the **buzzer** or the **bulb**?

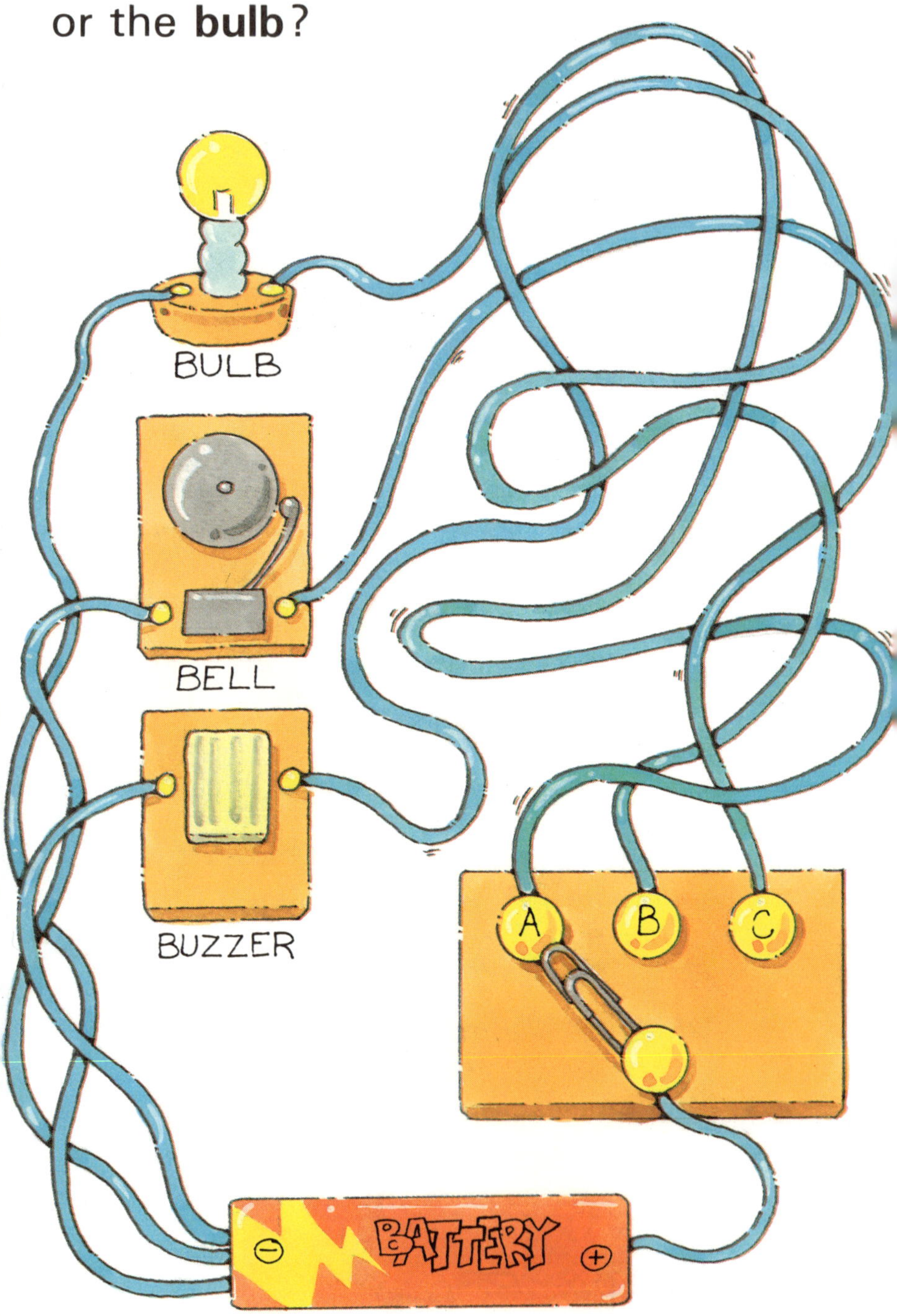

A ______________________________

B ______________________________

C ______________________________

7 Which of the objects below will **absorb** water? Mark them with a tick.

Make a list of other objects that will absorb water.

1) ____________________ 4) ____________________

2) ____________________ 5) ____________________

3) ____________________ 6) ____________________

8 Here is a **thermometer**. Some readings are marked with letters. See if you can match the letters with the sentences below.

1) A pleasant day in spring. ________

2) Freezing point of water. ________

3) Our body temperature. ________

4) A cold day in winter. ________

5) Boiling point of water. ________

6) A hot day in summer. ________

9 Which of these substances will **dissolve** in water? Mark them with a tick.

Can you think of other substances that dissolve in water?

1) ____________________ 3) ____________________

2) ____________________ 4) ____________________

10 If you were to spin these colour spinners what colours would you see?

1) ______________________________

2) ______________________________

3) ______________________________

11 Here is a family. How much do you think they each **weigh** and how **tall** are they?

The correct weights and heights are in these lists.

Weights: 15kg, 130kg, 50kg, 43kg, 85kg, 14kg, 6kg, 39kg

Heights: 165cm, 21cm, 242cm, 120cm, 365cm, 54cm, 140cm, 183cm

Dad ____________cm ____________kg

Mum ____________cm ____________kg

Lisa ____________cm ____________kg

Dan ____________cm ____________kg

12 Which candle will go out first, second and third?

A

B

C

1st__________ 2nd__________ 3rd__________

Why does this happen?

____

____

____

13 These model boats are in a race. Can you say in which position they will finish?

Write down the colour of the sail.

1st ______________________________

2nd ______________________________

3rd ______________________________

4th ______________________________

Do you know why?

____

____

14 Look at these children on the see-saws. Mark with an arrow the way the boy in red will need to move in order to balance the see-saw. The first one is done for you.

Try to find the **point of balance** of some of these objects:

A ruler, a pen, a fork, a book, a shoe and, with the help of a friend and a strong fence, yourself!

15 Have you ever looked at the **Beaufort Scale**? It describes the speed or **force** of wind. See if you can match the scale with the weather conditions.

0	calm	A	small branches move
1	light air	B	small trees sway
2	slight breeze	C	smoke rises vertically
3	gentle breeze	D	direction shown by smoke
4	moderate breeze	E	leaves and twigs move
5	fresh breeze	F	wind felt on face
6	strong breeze	G	large branches sway
7	moderate gale	H	widespread damage
8	fresh gale	I	whole trees sway
9	strong gale	J	twigs break off branches
10	whole gale	K	slight damage to buildings
11	storm	L	devastation
12	hurricane	M	severe damage

Which number is best for flying kites? ________

16 Which pulley system will make it easier to lift the weight?

Do you know why?

___

___

___